• A Haitian Story of Y

SéLaVi

That is Life

• by Youme •

Note to the Reader

The primary language in Haiti is Kreyòl, which has roots in French and West African languages. Words are pronounced phonetically, just as they are spelled. Sélavi means *that is life*.

Not so long ago and not so far away, people with guns could take a family, burn a house and disappear, leaving a small child alone in the world.

This child went north and south,
east and west. Here and there he found something
to eat and a place to sleep, but not a family
and not a home.

In the capital city of his country, the streets were
crowded with overloaded buses, cars with darkened windows,
and more people with guns. Angry faces shouted, "Move on,"
and "Go home." The child was too tired to keep going.
He sat on the curb with his head in his hands.

Suddenly, a hand was on his shoulder.
Was it a man with a gun? No, it was a boy
his own age, saying, "My name is TiFrè.
Have some plantains. What is your name?
Where are you from?"

The child ate hungrily but didn't answer.

"You can name yourself," TiFrè said.
"Like my name means Little Brother.
We could call you Hungry, Sleepy, or Little
Traveler . . . "

"I am all those things," the child said.
"And that's life." From then on they called
him Sélavi.

TiFrè brought Sélavi to the place
where he lived, a banyan tree near a market
square which emptied out in the evening. As the
sun went down, child after child came home with something
to share. Jenti, braiding Toussaint's hair, said, "I have some avocados
for everyone. They gave them to me for working at the restaurant."
Toussaint called out, "Mangoes for one and all. I was at the docks today."

Yvette and Espri introduced themselves. "Help yourself to drinking
water," Yvette offered. Espri smiled at Sélavi.

"And this is Mirror," said TiFrè, pointing to a child taking apart a
broken radio. He then placed fried plantains wrapped in brown paper
on a makeshift table. "We each bring back what we get during the day,
and we all end up with more."

That night they had enough to eat, a place to rest, and the comfort of each
other. As they settled down to sleep, Sélavi told of the men with guns and his
long run through the countryside. Then the others told their stories too.

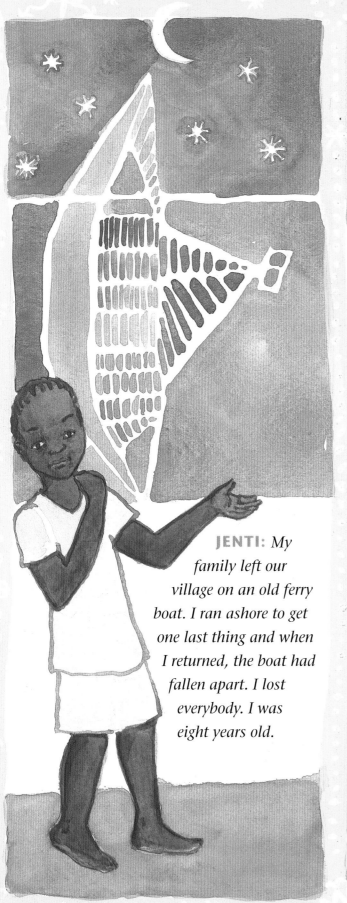

TOUSSAINT: *Man, I was nine and our house had three brothers, two sisters, four cousins, a grandpa, an uncle, two aunties, my mame and papa. It seemed like one dry bean for all of us, so I said, "This is more than one house can hold." I go back sometimes and make sure they are as okay as can be.*

JENTI: *My family left our village on an old ferry boat. I ran ashore to get one last thing and when I returned, the boat had fallen apart. I lost everybody. I was eight years old.*

ESPRI AND YVETTE: *We were sleeping when our parents woke us and told us to hide so we hid together in an empty oil drum. There was a lot of shouting and then silence. When we came out, there was no one. A family took us in to work for them, but they didn't care for us.*

TIFRÈ: *My mother moved us to the city where we knew no one. When she couldn't find a house, she made one from things she found. She got very sick and died. Soon after, my brother died too. I was too sad to cry right away.*

The next morning, and many mornings that followed, the children rose early to look for work washing cars, carrying water, cleaning clothes, asking people for money or food, and searching for useful metal or scraps that others had thrown away.

But then, one day a man in uniform pushed Sélavi roughly.

"All of you street children are dirty thieves," he said.

Sélavi was frightened. He ran back to the children's home beneath the banyan tree.

There were more angry faces there. One of them said, "We have chased away your friends. If we ever see you again, we will arrest you."

Sélavi ran down a side street and into a church. There he saw many families. Some of them seemed kind, but others were frowning because he had interrupted them.

A man was speaking to the people. "Alone," he said, "we may be a single drop of water, but together we can be a mighty river. We must help each other to become strong!" Sélavi called out, "I need help." Faces turned toward him. Sélavi told them about his friends and the men who had threatened him. An older woman said, "You are safe here." A couple stood. "Come live with us and be our son."

"Thank you very much," said Sélavi, "but what about my brothers and sisters in the street?"

The people talked to each other. "We can be the mighty river," they decided. They agreed to build a house where street children who looked out for one another could live. It would be a place to sleep in safety, to eat well, and even to go to school. It would be a home for Sélavi and his family.

The people called on everybody they knew to help build the house.

Some came with food and songs, others brought construction materials. When it was finally done, everyone continued to work together making food, washing clothes, teaching, and learning.

In the evenings they played soccer, told stories, and listened to the radio. The family grew. Is this the end? No.

Even though they had a home, there was still trouble.

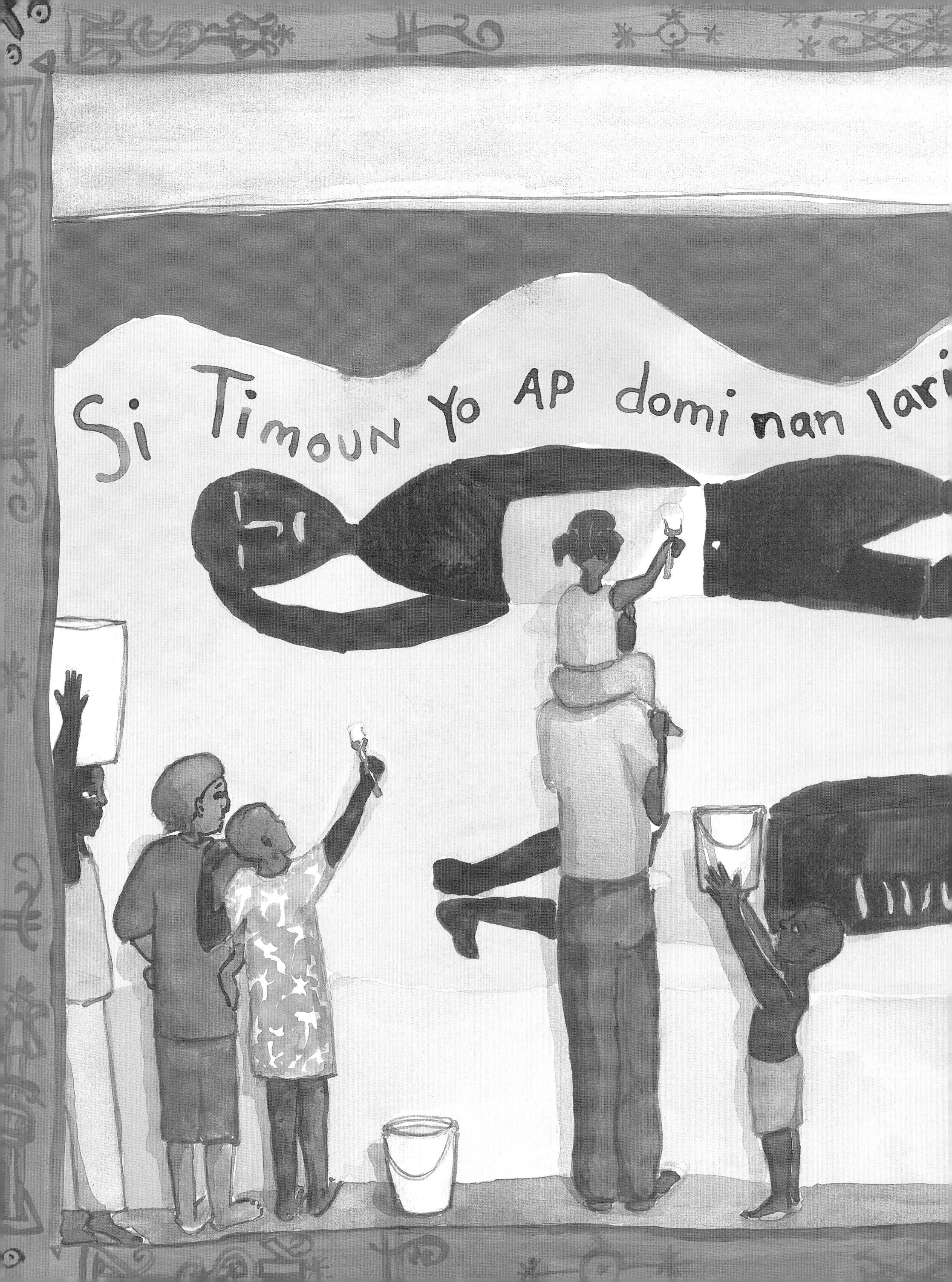

Si Timoun yo AP domi nan lari

Work was hard to find, and food was sometimes scarce. Sélavi and his family knew there were still other children who needed help. How could the river reach more people? They painted bright murals to let people know that they all needed help. This one says, "If children are sleeping in the streets, what are we doing for them?"

But the murals were painted out, and worse: some stood by and did nothing as others set fire to the building that had been a home for Sélavi's new family.

Is this the end? No!

The children were homeless again. Yes.
Everything they had worked so hard to
make had been destroyed. Maybe.
Someone had tried to
dry up the mighty river,
but that could not
be done!

*We still
have each other!
Let's rebuild our home.
And we still have our voices.
Let's start a radio station.*

Everyone knew of something to contribute. The house was rebuilt. Some found wires and abandoned equipment to repair, tape recorders and cassettes. Others worked to get a small transmitter.

Those who could read and write, wrote stories and news reports. Some made songs telling of their experiences.

deserves to be heard

And some built a tower to broadcast their voices to the whole country. "We will write our messages in the air where they cannot be painted out."

Even today they are being heard!
They continue to struggle but they know
they are part of a mighty river.
And now
so are you . . .

"All children need a neighbor or a friend who will keep an eye on them."

— RONALD JOSEPH,
a former resident at Lafanmi Sélavi

Is this story really true?

SÉLAVI is based on the experiences of homeless children in Haiti. Sélavi, TiFrè, their friends and family are real people. Together with the help of many other people, they started a home for children, called Lafanmi Sélavi, located in Port-au-Prince, the Haitian capital. The name of the home can mean both *the family is life* and *Sélavi's family*. Although the original shelter is no longer in use, another home was built farther away from the city center.

They also started a radio station called Radyo Timoun, which means *children's radio*. It continues to broadcast today. Radyo Timoun advocates for the rights of children with stories, songs and interviews. Its audience has become international as programs are recorded and played around the world.

© Youme

I first heard of the Haitian children's radio station when I was living in California. I told my friends that I wanted to make a book that would help to share this story in the United States and around the world. They got together to help me raise the money I needed to visit and interview the young activists of Radyo Timoun. There I met the children you have met in these pages—so many children working with each other and with adults to make a better life for everyone. I asked them what message they have for people in my country and they said, "Tell them we are here, that we are no less than wealthy children, and that there should be a place for everyone at the table."

The family of Sélavi is now made up of all people who live with hope and take action to help each other. It continues to grow and transform and affect changes in society. The book you are now holding exists because of all that we share. I am grateful to have this opportunity to honor the generosity of friends, the struggles and the courage of the children in Haiti, and the dedication of the adults who care about them.

Every child deserves to be heard.

Youme

THE **FAMILY OF SÉLAVI** is an extended family with a strong sense of community. Just as with any family, there are many chores, including washing clothes, preparing food and cleaning up after meals. The work is always more enjoyable when the tasks are shared.

WORKING TOGETHER also means playing and talking together. Like children everywhere, the kids in Sélavi's family have learned about life and community by working and playing and talking together. The home has also provided schooling and has helped its residents to become actively involved in making Haiti a better place.

"You're listening to Radyo Timoun, Port-au-Prince, Haiti."

O N CALL-IN SHOWS, like the one in this photo, a child phones in with a question for the young person who is on the air. Radyo Timoun is heard in all nine of Haiti's provinces every day. At the station, children from six to eighteen direct and produce radio programs which focus on the safety, health and social issues children face every day. The station has hourly scheduled news bulletins and on-air classes on subjects ranging from science and history to grammar. Youth correspondents report on events across the country. The station also plays music and presents radio dramas, giving the young people a voice to tell the story of their lives. The station is an important tool in educating the children about their rights, helping them to take an active and responsible stance toward their life within the community.

Tout Timoun Se Moun
All Children are People

My birthplace, Haiti, is a land of incredible beauty ...

My **NAME** is Edwidge Danticat and I am a writer. I was born in Port-au-Prince, Haiti, around the same area that this story takes place. Like many of Haiti's children, I was born poor, but both my parents had modest jobs, which made it possible for me to escape the fate of children like Sélavi, TiFrè and the others.

Edwidge Danticat's memories of Haiti combined with her deep love for all things Haitian have influenced her writing both in style and content. Her book *Krik? Krak!* was a finalist for the National Book Award in 1995.

My birthplace, Haiti, is a land of incredible beauty, but for many, it is also a place of great sadness. Located in the heart of the Caribbean, it shares the island of Hispaniola with the Dominican Republic. The Arawak Indians, who were the first inhabitants of the island, had named it Ayiti, meaning "land of the mountains." In 1492, Christopher Columbus landed on Hispaniola and soon the entire Arawak population was killed by the Spanish settlers. Later the French took control of Haiti and brought in slaves from Africa to work in coffee, sugar, and tobacco plantations. In 1804, the slaves revolted and won their independence, making Haiti the first black republic in the Western Hemisphere. Along with the American Revolution, Haiti's was the only successful rebellion in North America.

Haiti's connection to the United States does not end there. Haitians fought in the American Revolution, particularly in the battle of Savannah. And the Louisiana Purchase, the surrender of the state of Louisiana to the United States by the French, only happened after France's troops were weakened by their battles against armies of Haitian slaves. One of the first settlers of the city of Chicago was a Haitian man named Jean Baptiste Point du Sable and the great American naturalist John James Audubon was born in the lush southern region of Haiti, in a town called Les Cayes.

Since it gained its independence 200 years ago, Haiti has faced a series of man-made and natural disasters, including dictatorships, political violence and environmental depletion. When I was a child in Haiti, it was not uncommon, as the story describes, for soldiers or other people with guns to "take a family, burn a house and disappear, leaving a small child alone in the world." It was also not uncommon for a hurricane, a cyclone, or tempest to do the same thing, leaving behind land that could no longer grow food and nourish livestock and children who had no one to care for them.

These types of things continue to happen in Haiti, even today. This is why these days you're more likely to hear that Haiti is the "poorest country

in the Western Hemisphere," rather than "the pearl of the Antilles," as it was once nicknamed. Haiti is also, aside from Cuba, the place in the Caribbean from which most refugees arrive by boat to the United States. However, Haiti is a small and proud nation whose eight million residents share a glorious past, though at times a somewhat uncertain future.

It is this future that children like Sélavi, TiFrè and the others have inherited. Like Sélavi, most of the kids who end up homeless in Haiti's capital were born in the Haitian provinces. Forced to move to the city by a natural disaster or the death of loved ones, they end up on the streets, in market places running errands for a few pennies, washing cars in front of restaurants and nightclubs, or begging in front of airports, hospitals and churches. Underage and underfed, this is the only way many of them have of supporting themselves and, in some cases, even family members who depend on them. At night, these children sleep on the verandas of closed shops or on church steps and dream of a better life.

For a large number of them this better life never comes. Like their lost loved ones, some become crime victims. Others fall into crime themselves and are arrested and put in jail. However, some children do find hope. Some, like Sélavi, find other street children who look after them. Others are

photographs © Youme

taken in by relatives, or return home to the countryside, where they reclaim a difficult but familiar existence. Some very lucky ones even find havens in the city, places specifically created to help street children escape the terrible events that mark their daily lives.

Sélavi's story is based on a real orphanage in the Haitian capital called Lafanmi Sélavi. This orphanage was opened in 1986 by a Salesian priest named Jean-Bertrand Aristide who would later become president of Haiti. When President Aristide was overthrown by a military coup and sent into exile in 1991, the orphanage was bombed by the Haitian military. Four children were killed and the living quarters, which housed about 500 children, burned down. When Aristide returned from exile in 1994, he began a radio station for the children of Lafanmi Sélavi called Radyo Timoun—children's radio—which later blossomed into Tele Timoun or children's television. Both media outlets took on as their motto "The Voice of Haiti's Future" and continue to thrive today.

While Sélavi's is a story of hope, many Haitian children—about a quarter of a million of them—are still living on the streets. In a country where nearly 40 percent of the population is under 18, and a very large number of people live in poverty, one orphanage simply cannot house all of Haiti's neediest kids. Being a child of Haiti myself, I can only hope that Sélavi's story will be repeated in the lives of many other children, among them future writers, radio and television journalists, who will continue to tell—and show—their stories in such moving and powerful ways that the rest of the world will no longer be able to neglect them.

© Mahayana Landowne

Dedicated to my family of friends
— YOUME

YOUME—whose parents made her name up from the words "you" and "me"—is an artist and activist. She grew up in Miami, Florida, and Woods Hole, Massachusetts, listening to stories, reading her way through libraries, building tree houses and making books.

Youme's work has taken her to Nairobi, Kenya, where she wrote and illustrated for *Rainbow Magazine;* to Kyoto, Japan, where she worked as a graphic artist; to Santiago de Cuba as a participant in Inter Nos, a collaborative mural project; and to Port-au-Prince, Haiti, collaborating with children to paint murals and document their stories through drawings and the written word. She became a professional community muralist working with Precita Eyes Mural Art Center in San Francisco, California.

Youme makes her home in Brooklyn, New York, but she travels from there all over the world.

Look on our website under Teacher's Resources to find a guide for *Sélavi*.

Visit us at www.cincopuntos.com
or call 1-800-566-9072

Book and jacket design by
Vicki Trego Hill of El Paso, Texas

MANY THANKS to Jennifer Cheek Pantaléon for the use of her photos; to Jennifer's husband Guy for corrections on the text; to Edwidge Danticat for her help in elaborating on and affirming the story of Sélavi; to Greg Ruggerio for sending Youme our way; and to Joe Hayes, Diana Cohn, Mary Fountaine, Eddie Holland and Jessica Powers for their thoughtful consideration of this important book.

Sélavi, A Haitian Story of Hope. Copyright © 2004 by Youme Landowne.
Illustrations copyright © 2004 by Youme Landowne.
All rights reserved. No part of this book may be used or reproduced in any manner whatsoever without written permission except in case of brief quotations for reviews. For information, write Cinco Puntos Press, 701 Texas, El Paso, TX 79901 or call at (915) 838-1625.
Printed in Hong Kong by Morris Printing. Thanks, Suzy.
FIRST EDITION   10   9   8   7   6   5   4   3   2   1
Library of Congress Cataloging-in-Publication Data. Landowne, Youme.
Selavi, that is life : a Haitian story of hope / by Youme Landowne ; illustrated by Youme Landowne.— 1st ed.   p. cm.
Summary: A homeless boy on the streets of Haiti joins other street children, and together they build a home and a radio station where they can care for themselves and for other homeless children. ISBN 0-938317-95-4
[1. Street children—Fiction. 2. Homeless persons—Fiction. 3. Haiti—Fiction.] I. Title. PZ7.L2317354Se 2003 [E]—dc22   2003023885

Printed in Hong Kong by Morris Printing